It's TIME to...

RUN!

What ALL true believers will face
in this closing hour of church history

It's TIME to...

RUN!

What ALL true believers will face
in this closing hour of church history

By Robert Hooley

with Peter Brock

Authors' website: BethelBiblical.org
Authors' email: PRHooley1@aol.com; Hushai2048@aol.com

Mill City Press, Inc.
212 3rd Avenue North, Suite 290
Minneapolis, MN 55401
612.455.2294
www.millcitypublishing.com

FIRST EDITION
Unless otherwise noted, all scripture quotation is from the Authorized Version
(King James) of the Bible Cambridge University Press

1. Habakkuk 2. Prophecy 3. Last Days 4. Church 5. Old Testament
6. Chaldea/Chaldean 7. Eschatology 8. Final Word

ISBN-13: 978-1-937600-85-3
LCCN: 2012932565

Cover Design and Typeset by Wendy Baker

Printed in the United States of America

Table of Contents

Introduction

'Behold YE among the heathen, and regard, and wonder marvelously: for I will work a work in YOUR days, which ye will not believe, though it be told you'

These words are found in the beginning of the Old Testament book of Habakkuk, a powerful and amazing prophetic utterance that is only three chapters in length. But its message is ultimate.

The purpose of this book is to share what we believe is a profound word for the worldwide church of Jesus Christ in this closing hour of church history.

I direct a question to my long-time friend, Peter Brock. Why is it that over the past twenty-plus years this book has been such a challenge and focus of study in our lives? I believe I know quite well your answer!

The Hebrew name Habakkuk means to "embrace" something. This is certainly fulfilled in the way he imparts God's urgent prophetic pronouncement and sovereign purposes.

Over many years we have intensely studied and prayed that the Holy Spirit would give us proper understanding of these three chapters. Our hearts are certainly bonded and knit together regarding the importance of this special segment of God's Word. I had encouraged you to take the lead in putting something in print. You likewise exhorted me. I guess it is now time to jointly make the effort.

The previous declaration by Habakkuk in Verse 4 regarding the decadent state of unbelief accompanying this word of prophecy is compelling, as is the explosive challenge throughout this prophetic proclamation.

This ultimate statement about the utter unbelief in Habakkuk's prophecy must be seen in the light of his additional words in Chapter 2 (verses 2, 3) where we are told that at the time of the text's inevitable fulfillment there will be the occurrence of something truly unique – and unexpected!

There will be those to whom God will make the prophecy "plain." And, they will not only read and understand – but they will RUN with the truth. I believe it is time to RUN! Hopefully Almighty God will bless this effort to honor his Word and to encourage many runners.

—Robert Hooley
Lakewood, Colorado

Foreword

'You will not believe it!'

Why would God's word taunt anyone today who would read an obscure prophecy – from more than 2,600 years ago – by saying it will not be believed? Yet, ironically, it must be not just believed but "embraced" – more than life itself!

But, why trouble ourselves? There are many more convenient encouragements in the Bible to answer our worries in this pre-Apocalyptic world that seems on the verge of exploding.

If the people of Habakkuk's time wouldn't believe, why should we? The reason is that it was not written for them. Instead, it is especially written for us today. In fact, it says it applies not to ancient Judah and Jerusalem but to certain people who will be living in many places at a specific future time – and who are surrounded by hostile majorities who don't believe in God and don't like those who do.

At second glance, Habakkuk shockingly describes conditions today. Not just vaguely parallel to his or to New Testament times but in these careening, self-destructing Last Days. It becomes harder NOT to believe Habakkuk is foretelling God's terrible dealings with a people like us who least suspect they may already be confronted by severe and likely unprecedented testing. On one level, the glib headlines and commentators sensationally report the anticipated phenomena foretold by Jesus at the close of the age – terrorism, rebellion, civil upheaval, massed armies, wars, and impending environmental and cosmic events of horrifying magnitude. Divorces sky-rocketing. Morality plummeting. Betrayal. Corruption. Scandals. Meanwhile, politicians and even Evangelical ministers plead for "peace" – but civilization slides faster and faster toward catastrophe. But, this is all familiar cliché!

Again, how significant is Habakkuk for today? Nobody else seems to be talking about it.

Bob Hooley and I were sitting long ago at his dining room table with our Bibles open. He started reviewing the writings of Habakkuk ("embrace" in the Hebrew translation). I was nodding my head, but it was difficult to believe what I was hearing. I urged him to finish it up and put it into writing. We laughed, and in later months and years kept urging each other to do it, usually agreeing: "Why? Nobody's going to read it. Nobody will believe it. It says so." But, we never forgot it.

Then, he spoke about it publicly back in 2005 and sent me a tape. I listened. It was still hard to believe. Then, he did it again in mid-2011. This time, there was no doubt that we are clearly seeing it now – all around us.

"God has raised up an invisible army. And he has sent it against professing Christians and his church. A divine call for correction." Will you believe it – and RUN?

ROBERT HOOLEY

Take a deep breath...

—Peter Brock
Laporte, Minnesota

1

'Some kind of destruction,
some kind of loss'

Perdition. It is a word you don't hear much today. But it applies to believers in Jesus Christ. We have all heard the familiar verse in Hebrews which precedes it:

> *"Now the just shall live by faith. But if any man draw back, my soul shall have no pleasure in him."*
> *"But we are not of them who draw back unto perdition but of them that believe to the saving of the soul."[1]*

God is talking to believers, and the "just" are people who have been redeemed. They are saved, and they are called righteous. And it is clear that when the Bible talks about "living by faith" that the just are to live by faith in obedience to divine lordship. This is the main challenge that we face in our Christian life. We are redeemed, and therefore we must walk in obedience to God's lordship. This is the essence of truly living by faith.

We cannot "draw back." We cannot shrink back. And, we must not compromise our commitment of obedience to God.

If we draw back, then the Lord will "have no pleasure" in us, and will not say: "Well done, thou good and faithful servant."

Drawing back results in "perdition." This is a very powerful term and a hard consequence to face.

"Perdition" means some kind of destruction, some kind of loss. We are not necessarily saying somebody could lose their salvation. But, there is certainly implied some kind of severe loss.

Paul expresses it emphatically, writing that "when they say peace and safety, then sudden destruction…" comes to those who are not obediently walking with God.[2]

As believers, we all know we have to finish our course. We're in a race. And, God expects us to finish our course victoriously.

Now the statement in Hebrews about the just living by faith leads us back to the nearly identical warning that appears in Habakkuk:

> *"Behold, his soul which is lifted up is not*
> *upright in him. But the just shall live by his*
> *faith."*[3]

So, the just are those redeemed believers who are to

live by faith.

In a close study of this book, it becomes obvious that Habakkuk has a close relationship with the Lord. The Hebrew translation of his name means "embrace." He embraced the things of God, and God embraced him.

At the beginning of the vision there is clear evidence that God's people were consumed with pride. Habakkuk was writing firsthand about what he saw around him.

> *"The burden which Habakkuk the prophet did see."*[4]

In Habakkuk, one reason stands out about why people stray into disobedience. Their soul is lifted up. It is because of pride. They exalt self. They waver from being obedient to divine lordship in their daily walk. Habakkuk tells us that these are people who lift themselves up. Something is wrong in their heart. They're not upright. And, they're not pleasing to God.

They were not living by faith because they were not submitted to divine lordship as a way of life. The same is true today.

The key issue that God is pinpointing is pride. And, in both places the context links this truth to the End-Time. Not only is this made plain in Hebrews, but also throughout Habakkuk. It is our biggest root problem.

The word "pride" means to exalt self, to mount up, to pose majestically. Eventually it leads to haughtiness, boasting, and arrogance. But its root is disobedience to divine lordship. Notably, this is what happened to Lucifer and one-third of the angels who rebelled with him.

Pride was Lucifer's downfall, as he proclaimed from his heart:

> *"I WILL ascend into heaven...*
> *I WILL exalt my throne above the stars of*
> *God...*
> *I WILL sit also upon the mount of the*
> *congregation, in the sides of the north...*
> *I WILL ascend above the heights of the clouds...*
> *I WILL be like the most High..."*

In the space of a mere two verses in Isaiah, he repeated his boast five times – *"I WILL...!"*[5]

He had moved out from under divine lordship and exalted himself. And, this is when pride moved into the family of God. And, we know what happened next. It caused Lucifer and one-third of the angels to forfeit their position in God's kingdom, and they formed a rival kingdom of darkness. It was all because of pride.

An important statement in the book of Job helps us to understand the issue of pride and God's intention to "withdraw man from his purpose, and hide pride from man."[6] He wants to withdraw man from his own purpose and thereby to hide pride from him.

So, pride moves in when we put our purposes ahead of

God's purpose and we thrust ourselves forward, and we are not directed by the Holy Spirit. And, that is what happened to Lucifer – and pride has followed ever since in this universe.

The word "purpose" has to do with choice, intent and then action. It is something that comes out of the heart, and God looks on the heart. The issues of life come out of the heart – or where we make our deepest decisions.[7]

It must be added that "pride" is not always negative in character. It can be a force for righteousness. If we really are under God's covering and under his lordship, then we have a right to be proud of our Lord and of his Kingdom. This is a positive exertion of "pride."

But we must never forget that numerous prophetic texts reveal that pride is the ultimate issue about which God has to deal with men, and we know that pride led to sin and brought about the fall of mankind. God has to deliver man from pride. He has to hide it from us.

Though Habakkuk is a small book, it nonetheless elaborates on this important subject of pride and its relationship to believers in these Last Days. God tells Habakkuk and us that the effects of pride are visible worldwide and epitomize the hour in which we are living.

He is going to deal with this predominant spirit of self and bring discipline and justice.

"But the just shall live by his faith" – the faith that was once delivered to the saints. Jesus Christ, the same yesterday and forever. And it has not changed!

If our mind tells us differently, we are in danger of

crossing over a line and displeasing the Lord.

2

'Behold YE among the heathen'

How can an ancient Hebrew prophecy be important to the church today? More so, how and why is it indispensable – 2,600 years later – for contemporary Christian understanding?

The vision given to the prophet Habakkuk occurred when he was likely living in Jerusalem and was finally compelled to cry out to the Lord because the awful "burden" of what he saw and experienced was literally consuming him, physically and emotionally as well as spiritually.

Habakkuk writes at the beginning that he is further exasperated by the delay in receiving an answer as violence and rebellion were increasing and were out of control. He knew that at least a serious discipline was required, if not something more severe. Even judgment. The northern Kingdom of Israel had ended more than a hundred years earlier, and the southern Kingdom of Judah was being overrun by Babylonian hordes, commencing the seventy-year captivity.

The Hebrew word for "burden" implies something of "discipline" while the English translators use the more severe word "doom" in foreshadowing eventual judgment.

*"O Lord, how long shall I cry and thou wilt
not hear! even cry out unto thee of violence,
and thou wilt not save! Why dost thou show me
iniquity, and cause me to behold grievance? For
spoiling and violence are before me: and there
are that raise up strife and contention.
... The law is slacked ... There is no
judgment. For the wicked doth compass about
the righteous; therefore wrong judgment
proceedeth."*[8]

The word of God was abandoned. Society was lawless
and corrupt. Particularly, there was rampant injustice and the
believers were greatly endangered.

This summarizes how Habakkuk saw conditions
around him at that hour. But it had not gone unnoticed.
The Lord was already dealing with it. This was occurring in
approximately 604 B.C., even as Habakkuk was receiving his
vision and the first captives from Judah were being taken to
Babylon, or the modern-day area that principally includes
Iraq and Iran. Among these were Daniel and his colleagues
Shadrach, Meshach and Abednego, along with many more of
the young Jewish elite.

So, Habakkuk had long awaited an answer from
the Lord. But, the message that finally comes to him is an
example of a prophet abruptly changing the scene and time
to something global that is far distant into the future. There
was the historic reality that Habakkuk could see happening in

his hour. But, there was a far more important message being projected here which was the primary purpose of the vision more so than relating what happened historically in Judah.

Suddenly, having just started to describe the conditions around him, he launches into a detailed picture of the very days in which we are living:

> *"Behold, ye among the heathen, and regard, and wonder marvelously: I will work a work in your days, which ye will not believe, though it be told you."*

No longer are Jerusalem or Judah in view.

Instead, a people are in focus who are called "ye among the heathen."

And, God tells them to take note or to pay careful attention, or to "wonder marvelously." He is speaking into a future time period. "I'm going to work a work in your days. But you won't believe it even if it is told to you!"

This is an incredible statement. The scene is no longer Judah and Jerusalem, and the message is directed into the future to "ye among the nations." And to those people in that day is God declaring that he will do "a work."

Later on in the vision, the Lord says to Habakkuk that regarding what he is saying about the future scene that he wants Habakkuk to write it clearly. "The vision you've had, Habakkuk, I want you to make it plain so that some can run with it when they read it."[10]

This comes after saying that most people are not going to believe it, even if it is told to them. But there will be some that will read it – and they are going to run with it. Among all the Bible's prophetic writings, here is one about which they will say, "I'm running with it. It's life for me; it's so real."

Again, the time period Habakkuk is talking about is definitely in the future: "The vision is yet for an appointed time." It wasn't for Habakkuk's hour, but it is for the End-Time. The ones that see it and understand the message then will see the fulfillment of it.

Conclusively, we believe we are right now living in those days in this Church Age because Habakkuk emphasizes it will happen at the "end":

> *"For the vision is yet for an appointed time, but at the end it shall speak, and not lie: though it tarry, wait for it; because it will surely come, it will not tarry."[11]*

If God is going to make this real to a people that can "run with it," then it must happen in their time – at the "appointed" time.

Maybe up until this hour it has been tarrying. But, it is unmistakably exploding before our eyes in the day in which we are living.

As for this people described as "ye among the nations," God says that "I will work a work in your days," which he says will be a "wonder" and something "marvelous."

The Hebrew word here is *tamahh*, and it means God is going to do something "amazing" and "astonishing." This is why, generally, it is not going to be readily believed.

The identity of these people who "are among the nations" is also unmistakable. We remember that everyone in human society can be divided into three general segments. As Paul told the Corinthians, humanity consists of the Jews, the Gentiles, and "the church of God."[12]

Everybody is either born a Jew or a Gentile. Then out of those two groups comes the family of God.

Therefore, it can only be that these whom God is talking about and who are "among the heathen" or nations, is the church! This cannot be otherwise understood. It is the worldwide church in the End-Time. And a "work" will be done by God himself "in your days" that even though described beforehand "will not" be readily believed. But, there are those that will see it – and they will "run" with it!

In Habakkuk's day, we know that actual Chaldean/ Babylonian armies were used by God to invade and to bring discipline and judgment to the Jewish nation. Jewish scholars say that the word Chaldeah comes from the Hebrew *chesed*. They descended from Shem and became a powerful people around the 9th Century B.C. The Chaldeans were a proud people and were considered as Babylon's best. They were political leaders and wise men. We remember how Daniel had to contend with that Chaldean spirit derived from astrology and the worship of heavenly deities. They studied the constellations. Their "truth" was imparted from spiritual rulers in the heavenly places, from rulers of the darkness in this world spoken about by Paul. Much of the religious apostasy that came out of Babylon was passed on to the Eastern churches and eventually to Rome and Western Europe until it spread throughout Western society and has become the reality it is today.

But, this new Chaldean/Babylonian invasion is against a people other than the Jews. God is bringing a discipline to his church, which is worldwide, and his people are going to be required to make a choice. Further, these "invaders" are the spiritual "powers of darkness" identified in the book of Ephesians.[13]

God is doing the same thing in this hour to the church that he did in Habakkuk's time. We are undeniably living in this time of the great "falling way"[14] when God's purpose with those "living by faith" is to prepare a bride to be in love with the Lord Jesus Christ and to love his appearing. But, there are so few who believe this, although they say they are "believers."

And God is not any happier with this than he was with Judah and Jerusalem in Habakkuk's day. As then, the breakdown of society is distinctly visible today:

> *"This know also, that in the last days perilous times shall come. For men shall be lovers of their own selves, covetous, boasters, proud, blasphemers, disobedient to parents, unthankful, unholy,*
> *Without natural affection, trucebreakers, false accusers, incontinent, fierce, despisers of those that are good,*

Traitors, heady, high-minded, lovers of pleasures
more than lovers of God;
Having a form of godliness but denying the
power thereof… "[15]

God cannot be pleased with this. The flesh is running wild! People without self-control who may show a "form" or outward appearance of "godliness" or piety. But it is a caricature and false!

This was happening in Habakkuk's day. And God says, "it will happen again in another time period. It's going to be in the End-Time."

After many years of intense study, there is no question that this people "among" the nations is the church. Likewise, we know that God's judgment must start at the house of God.[16] Or, how can he judge unbelievers?

So, we are living today right in this End-Time scene that was revealed to Habakkuk.

3

Correction – or Judgment ?

A very important truth is disclosed by Habakkuk when the vision begins to unfold. We are told he perceives what is at the center of God's revelation:

> *"Art thou not from everlasting, O Lord my God, mine Holy One? we shall not die. O Lord, thou hast ordained them for judgment; and, O mighty God, thou hast established them for correction."[17]*

Habakkuk has realized, "God, you've let this happen; you've ordained it to happen. And, there are two things you want. You either want correction from your people, or you're going to bring judgment."

How many times have we felt God speaking into our lives that "correction" needs to be made? And, if we want to please him, we know it's important that we correct what is out of line. We know that he does not want to bring "judgment." He wants to bring correction.

God greatly desires to bring correction to America.

He doesn't want to bring judgment. And so, two choices were presented to his people 2,600 years ago in Judah – and today to the church.

In Habakkuk's time – when the first invasion actually occurred – God had raised up the Chaldean/Babylonian army.[18] It is the same today as the church faces a second invasion. God says, "I will raise up the Chaldeans, the Babylonians."

We recall that Lucifer is the king of Babylon. There is something sovereign about God letting the powers of darkness invade Judah as the Babylonians did against Judah, and now the church – to bring correction!

There is no formidable army existing today in the area of the former Chaldean/Babylonian kingdoms. Modern-day Iraq and Iran, which occupy that territory now, certainly have no armies that pose such a threat, especially world-wide. Instead, these invaders are powerful spiritual armies, as we know from Habakkuk and Ephesians.

They possess "hasty" and "bitter" spirits – realities that afflict human society today when "these spirits march through the breadth of the land to possess the dwelling places that are not theirs." They intend to dominate where and how we live. It is happening worldwide! "They are terrible and dreadful: their judgment and their dignity shall proceed of themselves."[19]

These are the same angelic and demonic powers that tore up ancient Babel. They know what they are doing. They know how to bring division. And, it fits the picture we see today. And God wants to use this now to open people's eyes and bring correction. We know that we want to walk with

God. We know he doesn't want to bring judgment.

Like in Habakkuk, there are scenes from the Bible where angelic powers are pictured as riding on horses. In fact, it is written that even our Lord will return on a great white horse. This is a picture of strength. These spirits involved in this End-Time scene are "swifter than leopards and more fierce than the evening wolves. Their horsemen spread themselves. Their horsemen come from far."[20]

We know that we wrestle against spiritual powers. Where do they come from? They come from "far," from the "second heavens." We don't wrestle with their flesh-and-blood agents or accomplices in society but with these influencing "principalities, powers, rulers of the darkness of this world, spiritual wickedness in heavenly places."[21]

What happens when these spirits come and take over? The same thing they were doing at Jerusalem and Judah in Habakkuk's time. The same thing they did at the Tower of Babel. They create division, confusion. That is what Babylon means – to create confusion. That is what Lucifer does.

"Their faces shall sup up as an east wind." Remember that the "east wind" represents judgment, prophetically speaking. They exert a spirit of judgment. "They'll gather the captivity as the sand."[22]

So often in church work today numbers mean everything. It doesn't matter how you get them. Just get numbers "as the sand" – and you're considered successful. But such success doesn't guarantee you're on the right pathway. It's more likely you are not.

Habakkuk argued, "God, you can't permit this to happen. These leaders in Jerusalem are making men as the fish of the sea, as creeping things. They're just ruling over them. They don't love them. They're using them. They take them up as fish and catch them in clever ways. They sacrifice to their nets and their methods, and they heap to themselves masses of people."

These spirits scoff at kings and princes. And toward true servants of God. They laugh at them. They mock them, scorn them. "They deride every stronghold." They'll do anything they can to tear up a marriage, to tear up a church, or tear up a family. "They heap dust and take it."[23] If anything is of the flesh – they promote it. Look at what is happening! People don't get married anymore. They just fall in love with somebody and start living together. They justify it as being "a different hour." They want to do things differently, they say.

This is what God was first showing Habakkuk about his time that historically happened in that era. And, God in his sovereignty is letting this happen again to get people's attention so that they'll make correction. He doesn't want to bring judgment.

It is so clearly the hour Jesus spoke about, as did Paul and Peter. All three talk about a tremendous falling away.

In the midst of such moral and spiritual collapse there is the abandonment of the faith once delivered to the saints – a message of holiness and separation. "We don't care what we do on the sabbath anymore." It's altogether different than a short generation or two ago when you heard church bells all

ROBERT HOOLEY

over town, and stores were all closed Sunday out of respect to God!

It's what is happening now. Many people are falling prey to these invading Babylonian spirits. They want the word of God and holiness to be thrown out the window.

Habakkuk further tells us about those in the church who will not believe his prophecy, as happened among doubters before the invasion of Judah:

> *Then shall his mind change, and he shall pass over, and offend, imputing this his power unto his god.*[24]

They will change their thinking and reject the warnings from God's word. This is crossing over a dangerous line. They don't believe the word of the Lord is to be taken seriously. The Bible doesn't mean the Bible anymore. And, they will fall for deception, and they are going to offend God! That is one thing that should never happen! But, they boldly accept strong delusion from lying spirits! They feel boldly "empowered" – a word you hear much of today. And they impute their ministerial successes and other impressive results as being from God. But, they are deceived.

But some will realize these methods are out of line with the Word of God. And, they refuse to do the same. They're determined to follow the real truth. They'll make correction in their lives, and God is pleased to see this.

We are living at the time when judgment is beginning

at the house of God.[25] Unbelief epitomizes this hour in history, and we are well into this worldwide scenario that was shown to Habakkuk.

Read this summary of the issues which displeased the Lord then – and displease him now:

❖ *"There are those that transgress by wine."*

> They are proud. They don't stay at home. They don't take care of their family priorities and responsibilities. They are out of control. You can't satisfy them. There is covetousness and greed. Their desires are enlarged to the size of hell and death. And they gather to themselves followings in all nations and heap to themselves all people. They are like Satan who had to be the top angel, the richest angel. They have to have the biggest ministry, etc.

❖ *"Woe to him that increaseth that which is not his."*

> God says to "take up a parable. And, I'll reveal what I'm going to do." They're impatient to grasp for more. They're among those who pad their pockets with thick clay pledges and suck money out of God's people for their own benefit. God says he will

deal suddenly and the situation will all rise up and bite them. They'll end up being vexed and stripped of everything, cheated by others. Their lusts to plunder were without limit and any means were used. And now it will be turned against them.

❖ *"Woe to him that coveteth an evil covetousness."* God must deal with his people about covetousness. They only care about their own houses. They just want to "set their nest on high." They want to be secure. They could care less about other people. They just want to be safe and to be delivered from the power of evil. But God says, "They have consulted shame to their own house." They've cut off many people. They could have been used to bring a blessing, to help people. Instead, they've sinned against their own soul.

❖ *"Woe to them that build a town with blood, and establish themselves by iniquity."* Habakkuk describes some of the great facilities that have been built in God's name but not for God's glory. "Even the stones and the timbers are crying out." They shout, "It's all fake!"

❖ *"It's not of the Lord of Hosts."*

Habakkuk says they are laboring in the very fire. They're losing any inheritance they could have had. It's being burned up because they won't make any corrections. They won't choose. They want an easy way. They're just wearing themselves out in vanity and emptiness. They induce others to follow their intoxicating, violent ways, adding to their shame. Inevitably, they try to justify themselves by false doctrines and boast about their ornate facilities of wood and stone as being worthy of worship in themselves.[26]

It is easy, then, to see all that it is falsely founded – upon a spirit of self. Remember, God sees the whole church scene world-wide.

4

'Can't there be some deliverance? Can't there be some revival?'

What was Habakkuk's reaction?

His End-Time vision contains five uses of "woe" – an archaic expression uttered when words fall short of describing great affliction, distress, misery, torment, pain, and suffering. Biblically, it is a term connected to judgment. For Habakkuk, there are vivid and hellish scenes of onslaught by the infamous Chaldean army, consisting of fearful, terrifying and dreaded hordes that would not only historically defeat Judah but also Egypt. The horrific effects of the vision on him were physical as well as emotional.

Habakkuk's "belly trembled." He was wracked by convulsions. "My lips quivered …and rottenness entered my bones.[27] It penetrated his innermost being and into the depth of his spirit.

This goes far beyond people who might bite their lips or chew their fingernails when confronted by a stressful scene.

It seemed that "rottenness" surged into his bones!

Some may have experienced a measure of this during a national tragedy or at the news of a devastating situation in somebody's life. All their strength is sucked out when they hear about it. "How could something like this happen to such a tremendous person ...or country?!"

Habakkuk said, "It made me tremble within myself and in my own soul, my whole being. And, it made my body shake." That's why God told him, "This is so astonishing and amazing that people will not believe it – even if they're told. They will not believe it. They will not listen." But still, he assures us there is a remnant of believers who will listen – and who will run with his vision.

"This is going to happen in a day of trouble." The prophet is saying all of this is going to happen, speaking into today. "You see the day of trouble coming. But, you're going to have to wait quietly when he cometh up unto the people. You're going to see it happen – if you're running with it."

This is not talking about the heathen but about God who will allow his own people – the church! – to be invaded. He says this so that we'll know that he is behind it, so that when we see this discipline, this correction happening, we'll know who is applying it.

God has armies of angels prepared to do his work. And when he speaks about judgment beginning at "the house of God,"[28] he will perform this himself.[29] His own troops will do it. He will bring it himself with his presence.

This almost exceeds our abilities to comprehend – let alone to "embrace" it. So, it is well understood why, church-wide, it will not be believed.

But, we can glimpse enough of the shaking worldwide today that we must acknowledge we are at least at the beginning of this time period. And, we must earnestly desire to remove ourselves from pride, from being unteachable, from arrogance. We must be teachable. We must deeply desire to be humble and lowly. We must aspire to receive correction.

We must remember that God is speaking expressly to us when he says, "Behold, ye among the nations." We should wonder marvelously. We should have this understanding about God when he tells us, "I am going to work a work in your days which you will not believe though it be told you." That is a very serious and sober statement.

This way or pattern of speaking by the Hebrew prophets – first declaring into their own time and then suddenly seeing and speaking thousands of years into the future – offers tremendous encouragement, whether predicting the restoration of the Jewish nation in the Last Days, or some prophecy about, say, America, or modern-day Egypt. It is truly wonderful and marvelous for our understanding and strengthening.

As for the actual administering of correction, God is not leaving that to the enemy. The work of the enemy up until now should be enough to have opened our eyes. But, God himself is NOW bringing correction by his troops.

It is hard to conceive how Habakkuk saw all of this with the full revelation of what we read now in the prophecy, but he surely realized that he had prophesied something very profound.

No wonder, then, that he knows he must pray, and we see at the beginning of the last part of the vision "A prayer of Habakkuk the prophet upon the Shigionoth."

"Lord, I've heard your message, and it made me afraid. You're talking about doom. And it put fear in my heart." And he next says what any good servant of God, man or woman, should do and say. He intercedes: "You're a merciful God. Can't there be some deliverance? Can't there be some revival? In the midst of this thing, in the midst of this promise of discipline and judgment to come, can't there be a move of God? Revive thy work in the midst of the years. In the midst of the years make known; in wrath remember mercy."[30]

This is the way we should appeal to God. Many times God has responded in marvelous ways to his servants. Moses pretty much saved the nation of Israel because he interceded and asked God for mercy. We should be praying the same kind of prayer for America today – and for the church! Therefore, we need for people to be alert and to know what is happening in this hour.

5

'What will people do if they forget their foundations?'

Concluding the vision, Habakkuk realizes an astonishing truth is unfolding to him that is literally shocking and upsetting to most people – and unbelievable.

He lists similar sovereign examples of God moving in time and eternity past. Great geological events are cited on earth, in the oceans and rivers, as well as throughout the cosmos adding to dealings among the nations and peoples through vast judgments and mighty works:

> *"God came from Teman,*
> *And the Holy One from mount Paran. Selah.*
> *His glory covered the heavens,*
> *And the earth was full of his praise.*
> *And his brightness was as the light;*
> *He had horns coming out of his hand:*
> *And there was the hiding of his power.*
> *Before him went the pestilence,*
> *And burning coals went forth at his feet.*

He stood, and measured the earth:
He beheld, and drove asunder the nations;
And the everlasting mountains were scattered,
The perpetual hills did bow:
His ways are everlasting.
I saw the tents of Cushan in affliction:
And the curtains of the land of Midian did tremble.
Was the Lord displeased against the rivers?
Was thine anger against the rivers?
Was thy wrath against the sea,
That thou didst ride upon thy horses and thy chariots of
salvation?
Thy bow was made quite naked.
According to the oaths of the tribes even thy word. Selah.
Thou didst cleave the earth with rivers.
The mountains saw thee, and they trembled:
The overflowing of the water passed by:
The deep uttered his voice,
And lifted up his hands on high.
The sun and moon stood still in their habitation:
At the light of thine arrows they went,
And at the shining of thy glittering spear.
Thou didst march through the land in indignation,
Thou didst thresh the heathen in anger."[31]

We recognize these as God's sovereign acts, some which happened with Israel, including from the days of Joshua when battling with the Amorites and needing more daylight for pursuit and their total defeat. The Lord responded with a sovereign and wondrous miracle: "The sun and the moon stood still in their habitation."[32]

Something similarly spectacular and sovereign from God can be expected in the future invasion into the church, remembering at the same time that his purpose is to help us, not to hurt us.

"Thou wentest forth for the salvation of thy people."[33] He wants his people to come out of tribulation. He knows how to deliver the godly out of temptation.

God wants something out of his church in this hour. He has a right to expect it. What's he going to do? God has to deal with wickedness in the midst of the church, in the midst of the worldwide church scene, just like he had to bring in the Babylonians and deal with Judah in Habakkuk's hour. He must deal with wickedness. He has to "wound the head out of the house of the wicked" if the "salvation" of his people is to be assured.

Such "wickedness" finds a place in the hearts of God's people – and it also can corrupt the heart of a nation that forgets its foundations. Certainly we are facing this tragic reality today in the United States.

"What will people do when they forget their foundations?"[34] It is already happening; we're seeing it.

It begins with breaking the commandments of God. The Ten Commandments are not allowed in public schools. They seemed to be laughed at everywhere else – or ignored! The idea of holiness is not even a punch-line!

The Lord concludes the prophecy of Habakkuk with encouragement for the righteous because he does not want to discourage us. He wants us to make correction. But he certainly wants to give us encouragement because we've all fallen short at times. And, he has had to deal with us and, thankfully, he has brought correction.

His final three declarations are momentous, and sustain and strengthen our spirits. He is speaking right into this moment of time and into our lives, and his advice to us is NOT to be overwhelmed or disheartened by what we see and experience.

"Although the fig tree doesn't blossom, and there's no fruit on the vines." People aren't interested in the fruits of the spirit. No, all that's important is to have a good time. Live it up! Holiness means nothing. Just kick it out the door. Fruits of the spirit? No, they do what they want. Holiness means nothing. Kick it out the door. Don't go to any church where fruits are important.

"The labor of the olive will fail." The Holy Spirit is denied his rightful place even though he is Lord in the church and your body is the temple of the Holy Spirit.

"There's no meat in the fields." There are not the kinds of results we should be getting. People should be bringing their neighbors to church to get them saved. We're not seeing what happened back in the earlier moves of God. Well, times have changed, they say, and we must "go the entertainment route" to reach the numbers, to attract crowds.

"The flock is scattered, and there's no herd in the

stalls." Just getting commitment to get the work done in the church is not as easy as it once was. So many have an excuse why they don't need to be in church on Sunday. They say it's a new day and a new hour![35]

When we see all these things happen, what are we supposed to do? Get discouraged? No.

"Yet will I rejoice in the Lord. I will joy in the God of my salvation. The Lord Jehovah is my strength. He maketh my feet like hind's feet. He maketh me to climb up on my high places."[36]

An unforgettable sight awaits those who go through the steep canyons on the way to David Ben Gurion's home in the desert near Engedi on the west bank of the Dead Sea. You can see these spectacular wild goats, or hinds, going up those mountain walls as if they have glue on their hooves.

For those who want to walk with the Lord Jesus – we can run in this hour! Like those hinds, you can ascend to those high places with God.

We can "rejoice" with true "joy."

The Hebrew translation for these two words – "rejoice" and "joy" – describe the experiencing of a great stirring in the heart, even a leaping or "spinning for joy."

In Mexico at the end of a service there was a group of spinners spinning for joy because they were happy in the Lord!

My pet Maltese would get so happy, she would run in circles. Spinning! Kind of the way when kids play soccer and they score a goal. They run in circles!

6

'Hell is not forever.' Or, is it?

A recent magazine article asked the question: "Is hell dead?"

It was based on the opinion of a certain pastor in our country who wrote a book that became popular and was a best-seller. It illustrates what Habakkuk talks about.

There are a large number of people in his congregation described as "non-traditional" and they emphasize "discussion rather than dogmatic teaching."

That's another way of saying: "We don't have to live up to the harsh interpretation of the scriptures."[37]

The writer of the article stated at the outset:

> "The standard Christian view of salvation through the death and resurrection of Jesus of Nazareth is summed up in the Gospel of John which promises eternal life to whosoever believeth in him. Traditionally, the key is the acknowledgement that Jesus is the Son of God who, in the words

of the ancient creed for us and for our salvation, came down from heaven and was made man. In the evangelical ethos, one either accepts this and goes to heaven, or refuses and will go to hell..."

This pastor disagreed:

> "He suggests that the redemptive work of Jesus may be universal, meaning that, as his book's subtitle puts it, every person who ever lived could have a place in heaven. ...This slim lively book has ignited a new holy war in Christian circles and beyond."

A leader of one prominent American evangelical denomination calls the book and its message "theologically disastrous. ...A young pastor was fired by his church for endorsing the book. Particularly upsetting to conservative Christians is that this book ...is not an attack from outside the walls of the evangelical city but from a ministry within it. A rebellion led by a charismatic popular pastor with a following."

Here's what the pastor that wrote the book said: "I have long wondered if there is a massive shift coming in what it means to be a Christian." He continues: "Something new is in the *air*." (Italics added) No doubt it comes from "far" – as Habakkuk told us already!

Here's somebody that says he believes in the atonement, but he has a different perspective of it:

> "Jesus the Son of God who was sacrificed for the sins of humanity and the prospect of a place of eternal torment seems irreconcilable with the God of love. ...Even from the time of the early Christian tradition in the first church, there were those who insist that history is not tragic. Hell is not forever."

"Love," the article contends, is going to "win out" in the end. And, the "gates of hell will not prevail against the church..." But, the interpretation boils down to the claim that God "is going to wipe away everybody's sin. Everybody will be saved..."

Jesus, according to the pastor, "speaks of the renewal of all things." Period.

But this partial quotation about the "restitution of all things..." is misstated from the book of Acts. He doesn't spell out what completes the rest of the sentence: "...which God hath spoken by the mouth of all his holy prophets since the world began."[38]

The article does not point out that there is not a single statement in the Bible, by any of the prophets, that backs up the twisted belief that "everyone is going to heaven."

In my opinion, what is really heartbreaking is that thousands in that congregation, including many young people, hear this kind of deception. But, it comes from the Chaldean spirits.

There is a tremendous spiritual shaking occurring today within the worldwide Church of Jesus Christ. This is clearly rooted in an all-out attack against the credibility, infallibility and supreme authority of the Bible: God's Word to all mankind.

This attack is an exact pattern of that faced by Adam and Eve in the Garden of Eden.

We are told that Almighty God placed a special tree in the midst of that beautiful garden. It was called "the Tree of the Knowledge of Good and Evil." Adam and Eve were instructed not to eat, or even touch the fruit of this tree. They were to freely partake and enjoy fruit from the other trees. The Lord clearly warned them that disobedience would result in a spiritual death. The scenario that followed is recorded in the book of Genesis and is well-known worldwide.

A wise and beautiful *cherubim* angel (Lucifer), now known as Satan, the Devil, enticed them to disobey God and partake of the forbidden fruit. This act of rebellion opened the door for Sin to enter into the Adamic Race.

We can rejoice today that our heavenly Father extends to all mankind a way of forgiveness of Sin, Salvation, and

Eternal Life.[39] The Bible reveals that Jesus, the Son of God, is the door whereby we must be saved.[40] Our confession of faith in his substituted death is the Bible way to Salvation and Eternal Life.[41]

The challenge from the book of Habakkuk facing believers today is abundantly clear. Questions and issues of life relative to Good and Evil are established by the Living God in his Word. He sets the rules, guidelines, and boundaries as to an abundant and fruitful life. Our place is to obey.

Making correction is an obvious key in this hour. We need to choose correction!

What happened to Israel is written as an example FOR US!

> *"Now all these things happened unto them for examples: and they are written for our admonition, upon whom the ends of the world are come.[42]*

It was the same when Israel was entering the Promised Land. They were to choose life or death – DAILY!

> *"I call heaven and earth to record this day against you, that I have set before you life and death, blessing and cursing: therefore choose life, that both thou and thy seed may live…"[43]*

7

'But, you've pushed me enough!'

There was a great move of God across America after World War II. Many famous evangelists brought the voice of salvation and healing that blessed many people.

The late Oral Roberts was one such man greatly used by the Lord, and the names of many others are easily recalled.

Huge meetings were held across the land, spreading to other countries.

My wife Carol and I with our two young daughters came to Denver in the early 1960s to begin a new church fellowship. I remember a very special older couple who began attending our services. They were very humble and the godly parents of a successful evangelist from the immediately previous years. But, we learned that they were deeply concerned about the current spiritual condition of their son. He was obviously hurting; suffering from depression, a broken marriage, and other setbacks. My prayer and desire was to reach out to him in love.

At lunch one day I asked him if we could set a date for him to speak in a service at our young, growing congregation.

I felt with all his experience this would be a special blessing for our people.

"Look," he answered, "I couldn't do it. But you've pushed me enough, and I'm going to tell you what I really believe now. I believe in 'the restitution of all things,' and I believe Satan will be restored. I believe hell is going to be wiped away and that God will restore everything."

He continued, inferring his statement about the 'restitution of all things' was backed up in the book of Acts but not completing that 'restitution of all things' is only part of what is written. The statement actually reads the 'restitution of all things, *which God hath spoken by the mouth of all his holy prophets...*'[44] (Italics added)

"There is not even one of the prophets who said or who would believe that way," I told him. He ended up rejecting everything we did to try to help him. Deceiving spirits can blind good people, and nobody knows if he ever got back on course. This was a heart-breaking experience for his parents and a shocking, learning experience for me.

Such convoluted misuse of God's word, like every other deception of the enemy, has its origins in pride.

And, like the church today which has its warning from Habakkuk, Judah was threatened with catastrophe more than a hundred years before Habakkuk's time. Unless they made correction.

The prophet Joel characterized how "invasion" was already prepared by the Lord's sanctified ones, capable of inflicting massive destruction and ruin – "very great and terrible!" – by "his army."[45] It would happen supernaturally. The entire nation would be involved. Nobody was considered immune because pride would be dealt with in everybody's life – unless correction was made!

"Blow the trumpet in Zion," Joel warns the people of God who are part of Zion. They are the ones who must hear the "alarm" that God is about to enforce his divine purposes and sovereignty. History shows that it was eventually enacted against Judah in Habakkuk's time – just as it is prepared for this final phase of the church age.

Concerning the potential of God's army to carry out divine correction, even severe judgment, Joel received a shattering prophetic utterance. It must be stressed that over many years I had both heard and read how many outstanding prophetic scholars also linked his words to an End-Time setting and reality in this present hour:

> *"A day of darkness and of gloominess, a day of clouds and of thick darkness, as the morning spread upon the mountains: a great people and a strong; there hath not been ever the like, neither shall be any more after it, even to the years of many generations.*
>
> *A fire devoureth before them; and behind them a flame burneth: the land is as the garden of Eden before them, and behind them a desolate wilderness; yea, and nothing shall escape them. The appearance of them is as the appearance of*

horses; and as horsemen, so shall they run.

Like the noise of chariots on the tops of mountains shall they leap, like the noise of a flame of fire that devoureth the stubble, as a strong people set in battle array.

Before their face the people shall be much pained: all faces shall gather blackness.

They shall run like mighty men; they shall climb the wall like men of war; and they shall march every one on his ways, and they shall not break their ranks:

Neither shall one thrust another; they shall walk every one in his path: and when they fall upon the sword, they shall not be wounded.
They shall run to and fro in the city; they shall run upon the wall, they shall climb up upon the houses; they shall enter in at the windows like a thief.

The earth shall quake before them; the heavens shall tremble: the sun and the moon shall be dark, and the stars shall withdraw their shining.

And the Lord shall utter his voice before his army: for his camp is very great: for he is strong that executeth his word: for the day of the Lord is great and very terrible; and who can abide it?"[46]

Mercifully, the Lord had held out his plea to Judah to make correction.[47] He is doing it again to the church, to individuals, and to America.

History tells how Judah evidently achieved some repentance – but not sufficiently to avoid destruction and the seventy years of captivity at the hands of the Babylonians.

It was the same issue for Judah then, as it is the same issue for the church and America today. It's the Eden issue all over again. Are we going to disobey God, as happened at the Garden of Eden? Or, are we going to come under his covering and be obedient to him? Will we choose to go the way of deception led by Chaldean spirits? Will we disobey and take the fruit off the tree?

More than ever, our younger generations today are assailed by a crescendo of lying Chaldean spirits as this final invasion is taking place today in the church and in our country and across the world. And, we must make profound correction quickly.

8

A Final Word

I will never forget an early college classroom experience. I heard a well-respected professor make this statement: "The Bible contradicts itself."

But, I don't remember him giving any specific examples.

His declaration made me feel very uncomfortable. I had a feeling that what he had said needed to be confronted. There was only one problem: I, for one, wasn't sufficiently enlightened in the scriptures to do so. This was truly a crossroads moment in my life. I left the classroom that day determined to spend some priority time reading ALL the Bible!

I am now blessed to be in the latter days of my earthly journey. The Bible has become a living book, a delight and joy for over fifty years. It is a continuing challenge of study, and I am still learning. I'm very thankful for the blessing of early, wise parental guidance.

I deeply appreciate the many faithful men and women who taught me respect for the totality of the Holy Writ, which tells me God has exalted his word above "all his name":

"I will worship thy holy temple, and praise thy name for thy lovingkindness and for thy truth: for thou has magnified thy word above all thy name."[48]

Also, he assures me his word is perfect:

"The words of the Lord are pure words: as silver tried in a furnace of earth, purified seven times."[49]

I have yet to discover that biblical contradiction to which my college professor was referring.

The book of Hebrews in the New Testament speaks about a great spiritual shaking in these days of the End-Time. We read how everything that can be shaken WILL be shaken.[50] But what cannot be shaken will remain and obviously be blessed.

Habakkuk's prophecy encourages sincere End-Time believers to whom God will give "hinds' feet" – and will be "runners" – to rise up into victorious "high places." Respect and obedience to biblical declarations is the key.

"Oh earth, earth, earth, hear the words of the Lord."
   – Jeremiah 22.29
"The grass withereth, the flower fadeth: but the word of our God shall stand for ever."
   – Isaiah 40.8
"Heaven and earth shall pass away: but my words shall not pass away."
   – Luke 21.33

It's time to – RUN!

Endnotes

1. . . . . Hebrews 10.38,39. Note: scriptures quoted throughout the text of this book may be paraphrased or shortened. The reader is encouraged to review them in their exact entirety.
2. . . . . I Thessalonians 5.3
3. . . . . Habakkuk 2.4.
4. . . . . Habakkuk 1.1.
5. . . . . Isaiah 14.13,14.
6. . . . . Job 33.17.
7. . . . . Proverbs 4.23.
8. . . . . Habakkuk 1.2-4.
9. . . . . Habakkuk 1.5.
10. . . . Habakkuk 2.2.
11. . . . Habakkuk 2.3.
12. . . . I Corinthians 10.32.
13. . . . Ephesians 6.12.
14. . . . II Thessalonians 2.3.

15. . . . II Timothy 3.1-5.

16. . . . I Peter 4.17.

17. . . . Habakkuk 1.12.

18. . . . Habakkuk 1.6.

19. . . . Habakkuk 1.7.

20. . . . Habakkuk 1.8.

21. . . . Ephesians 6.12.

22. . . . Habakkuk 1.7.

23. . . . Habakkuk 1.10.

24. . . . Habakkuk 1.11; cf. v.5.

25. . . . I Peter 4.17.

26. . . . Habakkuk 2.5,6,7,8,9,10,11,12,13,15,16,17,18,19.

27. . . . Habakkuk 3.16.

28. . . . I Peter 4.17.

29. . . . Habakkuk 1.6-10.

30. . . . Habakkuk 3.1,2.

31. . . . Habakkuk 3.3-12.

32. . . . Joshua 10.11.

33. . . . Habakkuk 3.13.

34. . . . Psalm 11.3.

35. . . . Habakkuk 3.17.

36. . . . Habakkuk 3.18,19.

37. . . . Quotations and the identities of persons named in the article are intentionally not divulged.

38. . . . Acts 3.21.

39. . . . John 3.16.

40. . . . Acts 4.12.

41. . . . Romans 10.9,10.

42. . . . I Corinthians 10.11.

43. . . . Deuteronomy 30.19.

44. . . . Acts 3.21.

45. . . . Joel 2.11.

46. . . . Joel 2.2-11.

47. . . . Joel 2.12,13,16,17,32.

48. . . . Psalm 138.2.

49. . . . Psalm 12.6.

50. . . . Hebrews 12.26,27.